Contents

Oak trees grow here

Oak trees grow in woods, parks and the countryside. In woods, oak trees grow tall to reach sunlight. In the open, their branches spread out wide.

4

The life cycle of an
Oak Tree

Ruth Thomson

Published in paperback in 2014 by Wayland,
Copyright © Wayland 2014

Wayland
338 Euston Road
London NW1 3BH

Wayland Australia
Level 17/207 Kent Street
Sydney, NSW 2000

Editor: Clare Lewis
Designer: Simon Morse
Consultant: Michael Scott OBE, B.Sc

Photographs: Cover (main) Nigel Cattin/Holt Studios
International Ltd/Alamy; 2, 7 Derek Croucher/Alamy; 22
Bart Elder/Alamy; 4-5 Edward Parker/Alamy; Cover (tr, cr,
br) 6, 8, 9, 10, 11, 12, 13, 14, 15, 16, 17, 18, 19, 20, 21, 23
(all) naturepl.com

British Library Cataloguing in Publication Data
Thomson, Ruth
    The life cycle of an oak tree. - (Learning about life cycles)
    1. Oak - Life cycles - Juvenile literature
    I. Title
    583.4'6
ISBN-13: 978-0-7502-8258-1

Printed and bound in China

10 9 8 7 6 5 4 3 2 1

Wayland is a division of Hachette Children's Books, an
Hachette UK company
www.hachette.co.uk

What is an oak tree?

An oak tree has **broad**, soft leaves and rough **bark** on its trunk. Its branches spread both up and outwards.

stalk

oak leaf

crown

Bark protects the tree from drying out and insect attack.

branch

trunk

All oak trees produce hard nuts, called acorns, that sit in a cup. Inside every acorn is a **seed** that could grow into a new oak tree.

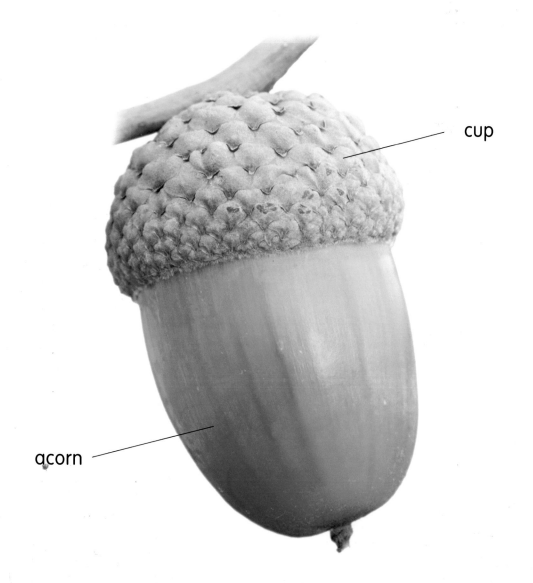

cup

acorn

Acorns

In autumn, acorns drop to the ground. Most fall in places where they cannot grow. Deer or birds eat many of them. Squirrels bury some to eat in winter.

In spring, buried acorns soak
up water from the soil. They swell
and their shell splits. A **root** starts
growing down into the soil.

Shoots

A small **shoot** pushes out of the soil and reaches upwards to the sunlight. Two small **seed** leaves unfold.

The shoot keeps growing.
By the end of summer,
it has about six new leaves.

6 months

Sapling

Oak trees grow slowly. The young tree is called a sapling. Every year it grows taller. Its **trunk** grows thicker. Twigs grow from the trunk.

5 years

The twigs grow longer and thicker
and become branches. More and
more leaves appear. **Roots** grow
deeper and spread wider, as well.

20 years

Tree

The tree is now well-grown. Its roots take up water, which travels up the **trunk** to the leaves. Leaves use air and sunlight to make food for the tree.

In autumn, there is not enough
light for leaves to make food.
The leaves change colour,
die and fall off the tree.

Winter buds

The bare tree rests all winter, while the weather is cold and windy, and there is less light.

Leaves and flowers start to grow on the tip of each twig. They stay tightly closed in the winter. Before these open they are called buds.

Flowers

In spring, buds open into leaves and flowers. There are male and female flowers. The hanging male flowers are called catkins. These are full of **pollen**.

Wind blows the pollen on to the female flowers of another oak tree. These will grow into acorns. By September, the acorns are fully grown.

Old trees

Oak trees can live for hundreds of years. Every year, new leaves, flowers and acorns appear. The **trunk** grows wider and the branches grow longer.

500 years

rings

Tree stumps

Sometimes, trees die of disease. Many are cut down. If you count the rings on a tree stump, you can tell how old the tree was.

Oak tree life cycle

Root and shoot
In spring, an acorn splits. A **root** grows. A **shoot** appears.

Sapling
Every year, the young tree grows bigger.

Acorn
After about 20 years, the tree produces acorns.

Flowers
Flowers appear on the twigs.

Glossary

broad   wide

bark   the tough outer covering of a tree trunk

pollen   the grains of powder in flowers needed to make new seeds.

root   the underground part of a plant that takes in water from the soil

seed   the part of a plant that grows into a new plant

shoot   the first stem and leaves of a plant

trunk   the thick woody stem of an adult tree

Index